KT-473-226

SINS
WE
ACCEPT

SINS
WE
ACCEPT

JERRY BRIDGES

NAVPRESS
Discipleship Inside Out®

NAVPRESS
Discipleship Inside Out*

NavPress is the publishing ministry of The Navigators, an international Christian organization and leader in personal spiritual development. NavPress is committed to helping people grow spiritually and enjoy lives of meaning and hope through personal and group resources that are biblically rooted, culturally relevant, and highly practical.

For a free catalog go to www.NavPress.com
or call 1.800.366.7788 in the United States or 1.800.839.4769 in Canada.

© 2014 by Jerry Bridges

All rights reserved. No part of this publication may be reproduced in any form without written permission from NavPress, P.O. Box 35001, Colorado Springs, CO 80935. www.navpress.com

NAVPRESS and the NAVPRESS logo are registered trademarks of NavPress. Absence of ® in connection with marks of NavPress or other parties does not indicate an absence of registration of those marks.

ISBN-13: 978-1-61291-600-2

Some of the anecdotal illustrations in this book are true to life and are included with the permission of the persons involved. All other illustrations are composites of real situations, and any resemblance to people living or dead is coincidental.

All Scripture quotations in this publication are taken from the Holy Bible, English Standard Version® (ESV®), copyright © 2001 by Crossway, a publishing ministry of Good News Publishers. ESV® Text Edition: 2011. Used by permission. All rights reserved.

Printed in the United States of America

1 2 3 4 5 6 7 8 / 19 18 17 16 15 14

Contents

The Disappearance of Sin

A pastor invited the men in his church to join him in a prayer meeting. Rather than praying about the spiritual needs of the church as he expected, all of the men, without exception, prayed about the sins of the culture, primarily abortion and homosexuality. Finally, the pastor, dismayed over the apparent self-righteousness of the men, closed the prayer meeting with the well-known prayer of the tax collector: "God, be merciful to me, a sinner!" (Luke 18:13).

The attitude toward sin reflected in the prayers of those men seems all too prevalent within our conservative, evangelical circles. Of course, this is a broad-brush observation, and there are many happy exceptions. But on the whole, we appear to be more concerned about the sins of society than we are the sins of the saints. In fact, we often indulge in what I call the "respectable" or "acceptable" sins without any sense of sin. Our gossip or unkind words about a brother or sister in Christ roll easily off our tongues without any awareness of wrongdoing. We harbor hurts over wrongs long past without any effort to forgive as God has forgiven us. We look down our religious noses at "sinners" in society without any sense of a humble "there but for the grace of God go I" spirit.

We were incensed, and rightfully so, when a major denomination ordained a practicing homosexual as a bishop. Why do we not also mourn over our selfishness, our critical spirit, our impatience, and our anger? It's easy to let ourselves off the hook by saying that these sins are not as bad as the flagrant ones of society. But God has not given us the authority to establish values for different sins. Instead He says through James, "Whoever keeps the whole law but fails in one point has become accountable for [is guilty of] all of it" (James 2:10). That Scripture is difficult for us to understand because we think in terms of individual laws and their respective penalties. But God's Law is seamless. The Bible speaks not of God's *laws*, as if many of them, but of God's *Law* as a single whole. When a person commits murder, he breaks God's Law. When a Christian lets speech that tends to tear down another person come out of his mouth, he breaks God's Law.

Of course, we need to acknowledge that some sins are more serious than others. I would rather be guilty of a lustful look than of adultery. Yet Jesus said that with that lustful look, I have actually committed adultery in my heart. I would rather be angry at someone than murder that person. Yet Jesus said that whoever murders and whoever is angry with his brother are both liable to judgment (see Matthew 5:21-22). The truth is, all sin is serious because all sin is a breaking of God's Law.

The apostle John wrote, "Sin is lawlessness" (1 John 3:4). All sin, even sin that seems so minor in our eyes, is lawlessness. It is not just the breaking of a single command; it is a complete disregard for the Law of God, a deliberate rejection of His moral will in favor of fulfilling one's own desires. In our human values of civil laws, we draw a huge distinction between an otherwise "law-abiding citizen" who gets an occasional traffic ticket and a person who lives a "lawless" life in contempt and utter disregard for all laws. But the Bible does not seem to make that distinction. Rather, it simply says sin — all sin without distinction — is lawlessness.

In Greek culture, *sin* originally meant to "miss the mark" — to miss the center of the target. Therefore, sin was considered a miscalculation or failure to achieve. There is some truth in that idea even today, as when a person is genuinely repentant over some sinful behavior and is earnestly seeking to overcome it but still fails frequently. He wants to hit the bull's-eye every time but can't seem to pull it off. Usually, however, our sinful actions stem not from a failure to achieve but rather from an inner urge to fulfill our own desires. As James wrote, "Each person is tempted when he is lured and enticed by his own desire" (James 1:14). We gossip or lust because of the sinful pleasure we get out of it. At that time, the lure of that momentary pleasure is stronger than our desire to please God.

Sin is sin. Even those sins that I call "the acceptable sins of the saints" — those sins that we tolerate in our lives — are serious in God's eyes. Our religious pride, our critical attitudes, our unkind speech about others, our impatience and anger, even our anxiety (see Philippians 4:6) — all of these are serious in the sight of God.

The apostle Paul, in stressing the need to seek justification by faith in Christ alone, quoted from the Old Testament, "Cursed be everyone who does not abide by all things written in the Book of the Law, and do them" (Galatians 3:10). That is a perfectly exacting standard of obedience. In academic terms, that means that a 99 on a final exam is a failing grade. It means that a misplaced comma in an otherwise fine term paper would garner an "F." Now, happily, Paul goes on to assure us that Christ has "redeemed us [all who trust in Him as their redeemer] from the curse of the law by becoming a curse for us" (verse 13). But the fact still remains that the seemingly minor sins we tolerate in our lives do indeed deserve the curse of God.

Yes, the whole idea of sin may have disappeared from our culture. It may have been softened in many of our churches so as not to make the audiences uncomfortable. And, sad to say, the concept of sin among many conservative Christians has been essentially redefined to cover only the obviously gross sins of our society. The result, then, is that for many morally upright believers, the awareness of personal sin has effectively disappeared from their consciences. But it has not disappeared from the sight of God. Rather, all sins — both the so-called respectable sins of the saints, which we too often tolerate, and the flagrant sins of society, which we are quick to condemn — are a disregard for the Law of God and are reprehensible in His sight. Both deserve the curse of God.

If this observation seems too harsh and too sweeping an indictment of believers, let me hasten to say that there are many godly, humble people who are happy exceptions. In fact, the paradox is that those whose lives most reflect the fruit of the Spirit are usually those who are most keenly aware of and groan inwardly over these so-called acceptable sins in their own lives. But there is also a vast multitude who are quite judgmental toward the grosser sins of society but who seem pridefully unaware of their own personal sins. And a lot of us live somewhere in between. But the point is that all of our sin — wherever we may be on the spectrum of personal awareness of it in our lives — is reprehensible in the sight of God and deserving of His judgment.

Sin is much more than wrong actions, unkind words, or even those evil thoughts we never express. Sin is a principle or moral force in our hearts, our inner being. Our sinful actions, words, and thoughts are simply expressions of the principle of sin residing within us, even in those of us whose hearts have been renewed. The apostle Paul calls this principle the *flesh* (or *sinful nature* in some Bible translations). The flesh is such a reality that Paul sometimes personifies it (see, for example, Romans 7:8-11; Galatians 5:17).

Now, here is the unvarnished truth that we need to lay to heart. Even though our hearts have been renewed, even though we have been freed from the absolute dominion of sin, even though God's Holy Spirit dwells within our bodies, this principle of sin still lurks within us and wages war against our souls. It is the failure to recognize the awful reality of this truth that provides the fertile soil in which our "respectable" or "acceptable" sins grow and flourish.

We who are believers tend to evaluate our character and conduct relative to the moral culture in which we live. Because we usually live at a higher moral standard than society at large, it is easy for us to feel good about ourselves and assume that God feels that way also. We fail to reckon with the reality of sin still dwelling within us.

Another good descriptive term is *subtle sins*. The word *subtle* has a wide variety of meanings, some positive, as in the subtle shades of blue in a painting. But often it has a strong negative connotation to mean wily, crafty, insidious, or treacherous. That is the sense of the word in the expression *subtle sins*. The acceptable sins are subtle in the sense that they deceive us into thinking they are not so bad, or not thinking of them as sins, or, even worse, not even thinking about them at all! Yes, some of our refined sins are so subtle that we commit them without even thinking about them, either at the time or afterward. We often live in unconscious denial of our "acceptable" sins.

We present-day believers have, to some extent, been influenced by the "feel good about myself" philosophy of our times. By contrast, believers in the Puritan era of the seventeenth century had a different view of themselves. They feared the reality of sin still dwelling in them. I have in my library four books on sin by pastors of that era. Here are their titles:

- *The Sinfulness of Sin*
- *The Mischief of Sin*

- *The Anatomy of Secret Sins*
- *The Evil of Evils or The Exceeding Sinfulness of Sin*

These pastors all saw sin for what it actually is: a diabolical force within us. Ralph Venning, the author of *The Sinfulness of Sin*, uses especially colorful (in the negative sense) words to describe sin. Over the space of only a few pages, he says that sin is vile, ugly, odious, malignant, pestilent, pernicious, hideous, spiteful, poisonous, virulent, villainous, abominable, and deadly.

Take a few moments to ponder those words so as to get the full impact of them. Those words describe not just the scandalous sins of society but also the respectable sins we tolerate in our own lives. Think of such tolerated sins as impatience, pride, resentment, frustration, and self-pity. Do they seem odious and pernicious to you? They really are. To tolerate those sins in our spiritual lives is as dangerous as to tolerate cancer in our bodies. Seemingly small sins can lead to more serious ones. Lustful looks often lead to pornography addiction and perhaps even adultery. Murder often has its genesis in anger, which grows into bitterness, then hatred, and finally murder.

About this time, you may be tempted to throw this booklet across the room. You didn't pick it up to be condemned or have your subtle sins exposed. So far everything in this book seems dark and dismal. You want to be encouraged, not condemned. If you feel that way, I appeal to you to stay with me. We are indeed going to get to some good news later on. But for now, we've got to continue to explore the bad news. In fact, it is going to get worse. When we see how really bad the bad news is, we'll be in a better position to appreciate how really good the good news is.

So how does the already bad news get worse? So far we've looked at our sin as it affects us. We've seen its malignant tendency in our lives and the lives of others around us. The more important issue, however, is how our sin affects God. Someone has described sin as cosmic treason. If that seems like an overstatement, consider that the word *transgressions* in the Bible, as seen in Leviticus 16:21, actually means rebellion against authority—in this case, God's authority. So when I gossip, I am rebelling against God. When I harbor resentful thoughts toward someone instead of forgiving him or her in my heart, I am rebelling against God.

In Isaiah 6:1-8, the prophet Isaiah sees a vision of God in His absolute majesty. He hears angelic beings calling out, "Holy, holy, holy is the LORD of hosts; the whole earth is full of his glory!" (verse 3). Any Jew would have understood that the threefold repetition of the word *holy* is intended to convey the highest possible degree of holiness. In other words, God is said to be infinitely holy. But what does it mean to say that God is infinitely holy? Certainly it speaks of His absolute moral purity, but it means much more than that. Primarily, the word *holy*, when used of God, speaks of His infinite, transcendent majesty. It speaks of His sovereign reign over all His creation. Therefore, when we sin, when we violate the Law of God in any way, be it ever so small in our eyes, we rebel against the sovereign authority and transcendent majesty of God. To put it bluntly, our sin is an assault on the majesty and sovereign rule of God. It is indeed cosmic treason.

Let's continue with the bad news. Remember the story of David's sin of adultery with Bathsheba and then his arranging the death of her husband, Uriah, to try to cover up his adultery? God was displeased, to put it mildly, and sent Nathan the prophet to confront David about his sin. Here are Nathan's words:

> Why have you *despised* the word of the LORD, to do what is evil in his sight? You have struck down Uriah the Hittite with the sword and have taken his wife to be your wife and have killed him with the sword of the Ammonites. Now therefore the sword shall never depart from your house, because you have *despised* me and have taken the wife of Uriah the Hittite to be your wife. (2 Samuel 12:9-10, emphasis added)

Note the use of the word *despised* in both verses 9 and 10. In the first instance, David despises the word (the Law) of the Lord. In the second instance, God, speaking through Nathan, says, "You have despised me." We see from this that sin is a despising of the Law of God. But we also see that to despise God's Law is to despise Him. It is easy for us to think that David's sin truly was grievous and fail to grasp the application of Nathan's words to ourselves. But as we have already seen, all sin, whether large or small in our eyes, is against God. Therefore, when I indulge in any of the so-called acceptable sins, I am despising not only God's Law but also, at the same time, God Himself. Think about that the next time you're tempted to speak critical or unkind words about someone.

We're not through yet. There's still more bad news. In the context of exposing sin in our relationships with one another (see Ephesians 4:25-32), Paul says, "Do not grieve the Holy Spirit of God, by whom you were sealed for the day of redemption" (verse 30). When we think of our sin as rebellion against God's sovereign authority and a despising of both His Law and His person, we are viewing God in His rightful role as our ruler and judge. But when we see our sin as grieving the Holy Spirit — that is, as grieving God — we are viewing God as our redeemer and Father. Our sin grieves our heavenly Father. Whether we are unkind to someone else or unforgiving when someone is unkind to us, we grieve our Father's heart.

Not only do we grieve our heavenly Father with our sin, we also presume on His grace. Paul wrote that God has "[forgiven] our trespasses, according to the riches of his grace" (Ephesians 1:7). That is a blessed truth, but sin, in its subtle deceitfulness, will suggest to us that our unkind words and resentful thoughts don't matter because God has forgiven them. Forgiveness, however, does not mean overlooking or tolerating our sin. God never does that. Instead, God *always* judges sin. But in our case (that is, the case of all who trust in Jesus as their Savior), God has judged our sin in the person of His Son. As the prophet Isaiah wrote, "All we like sheep have gone astray; we have turned — every one — to his own way; and the Lord has laid on him the iniquity of us all" (Isaiah 53:6). Shall we presume on God's grace by tolerating in ourselves the very sin that nailed Christ to the cross?

God knows our every thought; He hears our words before we even speak them and sees our every deed. He even searches our motives, for Paul wrote that when the Lord comes, He "will disclose the purposes [motives] of the heart" (1 Corinthians 4:5).

This means that all our rebellion, all our despising of God and His Law, all our grieving His Holy Spirit, all our presuming on His grace, all our sin, are done openly in the very presence of God. It's as if we are acting out all of our sin before Him as He sits on His royal throne.

The Root Sin: Ungodliness

When I talk about specific areas of acceptable sins, one comment I often hear is that pride is the root cause of all of them. While I agree that pride does play a major role in the development and expression of our subtle sins, I believe there is another sin that is even more basic, more widespread, and more apt to be the root cause of our other sins: the sin of *ungodliness*, of which we are all guilty to some degree.

Does that statement surprise you, or maybe even offend you? We don't think of ourselves as ungodly. After all, we *are*

Christians; we are not atheists or wicked people. We attend church, avoid scandalous sins, and lead respectable lives. In our minds, the ungodly folks are the ones who live truly wicked lives. How, then, can I say that we believers are all, to some extent, ungodly?

Ungodliness may be defined as living one's everyday life with little or no thought of God, or of God's will, or of God's glory, or of one's dependence on Him. You can readily see, then, that someone can lead a respectable life and still be ungodly in the sense that God is essentially irrelevant in his or her life. We rub shoulders with such people every day in the course of our ordinary activities. They may be friendly, courteous, and helpful to other people, but God is not at all in their thoughts. They may even attend church for an hour or so each week but then live the remainder of the week as if God doesn't exist. They are not wicked people, but they are ungodly.

The sad fact is that many of us who are believers tend to live our daily lives with little or no thought of God. We may even read our Bibles and pray for a few minutes at the beginning of each day, but then we go out into the day's activities and basically live as though God doesn't exist. We seldom think of our dependence on God or our responsibility to Him. We might go for hours with no thought of God at all. In that sense, we are hardly different from our nice, decent, but unbelieving neighbor. God is not at all in his thoughts and is seldom in ours.

One cannot carefully read the New Testament without recognizing how far short we come in living out a biblical standard of godliness. I referred earlier to our seldom thinking of our dependence on God. In that regard, consider these words from James:

> Come now, you who say, "Today or tomorrow we will go into such and such a town and spend a year there and trade and make a profit" — yet you do not know what tomorrow will bring. What is your life? For you are a mist that appears for a little time and then vanishes. Instead you ought to say, "If the Lord wills, we will live and do this or that." (4:13-15)

James does not condemn these people for making plans or even planning to set up a business and make a profit. What he condemns is their planning that does not acknowledge their dependence on God. We make plans all the time. In fact, we couldn't live or accomplish the most mundane duties of life without some degree of planning. But so often we act like the people James addressed. We, too, make our plans without recognizing our utter dependence on God to carry them out. That is one expression of ungodliness.

In the same way, we seldom think of our accountability to God and our responsibility to live according to His moral will as revealed to us in Scripture. It's not that we are living obviously sinful lives; it's just that we seldom think about the will of God and, for the most part, are content to avoid obvious sins. Yet Paul wrote to the Colossian believers,

> We have not ceased to pray for you, asking that you may be filled with the knowledge of his will in all spiritual wisdom and understanding, so as to walk in a manner

worthy of the Lord, fully pleasing to him, bearing fruit in every good work and increasing in the knowledge of God. (Colossians 1:9-10)

Notice how God-centered that prayer is. Paul wanted his hearers to be full of the knowledge of God's will — that is, His moral will. He desired that they live lives worthy of God and fully pleasing to Him, and he prays to that end. That is God-centered praying. Paul wanted the Colossians to be godly people.

How does Paul's prayer for the Colossians compare with our prayers for ourselves, our families, and our friends? Do our prayers reflect a concern for God's will and God's glory and a desire that our lives will be pleasing to God? Or are our prayers more of a do-list we present to God, asking Him to intervene in the various health and financial needs of family and friends? It is not wrong to bring these temporal needs to God. In fact, that's one way we can acknowledge our daily dependence on Him. But if that's all we pray about, we are merely treating God as a "divine bellhop." Our prayers are essentially human-centered, not God-centered, and in that sense, we are ungodly to some degree.

For Paul, all of life is to be lived out in the presence of God with an eye to pleasing Him. For example, note how Paul instructed the slaves in the Colossian church (very likely a large part of the congregation) as to how to serve their masters in a godly fashion:

> Obey in everything those who are your earthly masters, not by way of eye-service, as people-pleasers, but with sincerity of heart, fearing the Lord. Whatever you do, work heartily, as for the Lord and not for men, knowing that from the Lord you will receive the inheritance as your reward. You are serving the Lord Christ. (Colossians 3:22-24)

His admonition to "work heartily, as for the Lord and not for men" (verse 23) provides us with a principle by which we are to seek to live godly lives in the context of our vocations or professions. Yet how many believers seek to live by this principle in their daily lives? Do we not approach our vocations much like our unbelieving and ungodly coworkers who work purely for themselves, their promotions, and their pay raises, with no thought of pleasing God?

For the godly person, God is the center and focal point of his or her life. Every circumstance and every activity of life, whether in the temporal or spiritual realm, is viewed through the lens of this God-centeredness; however, such a God-centeredness can be developed only in the context of an ever-growing intimate relationship with God. No one can genuinely desire to please God or glorify Him apart from such a relationship.

Sins of the tongue — such as gossip, sarcasm, and other unkind words to or about another person — cannot thrive in awareness that God hears every word we speak. The reason we sin with our tongues is due to the fact that we are to some degree ungodly. We don't think of living every moment of our lives in the presence of an all-seeing, all-hearing God.

I believe that all our other acceptable sins can ultimately be traced to this root sin of ungodliness. To use a tree as an illustration, we can think of all our sins, big and small, growing out of the trunk of pride. I have in mind such sins as anxiety, discontent, unthankfulness, lack of self-control, impatience, anger, judgmentalism, envy, jealousy, and so forth. But that which sustains the life of the tree is the root system, in this case the root of ungodliness. It is ungodliness that ultimately gives life to our more visible sins.

If ungodly habits of thinking, then, are so commonplace with us, how can we deal with this sin? How can we become more godly in our daily lives? Paul wrote to Timothy, "Train yourself for godliness" (1 Timothy 4:7). The word *train* comes from the athletic culture of that day and refers to the practice athletes went through daily to prepare themselves to compete in their athletic contests. It implies, among other things, commitment, consistency, and discipline.

The Remedy for Sin

John Newton, who wrote the much-loved hymn "Amazing Grace," was earlier in his life a slave trader and even captain of a ship transporting captured Africans to America. For medical reasons, he left the seafaring life, became a customs officer, studied theology, and eventually became a minister. However, even as a minister, Newton never forgot the horrible nature of his sin as a slave trader. At the end of his life, Newton said to a friend, "My memory is nearly gone; but I remember two things: that I am a great sinner, and that Christ is a great Savior."[1]

Centuries before, Saul of Tarsus, who became the apostle Paul, was also guilty of grievous sins. Acts 7:54–8:1 describes his complicity in the stoning of Stephen; then in Acts 9:1-2, we read of his personal involvement in persecuting believers. Toward the end of his life, Paul described himself in those earlier days as "a blasphemer, persecutor, and insolent opponent [of Christ]" (1 Timothy 1:13). But in that same context, he could also say, "Christ Jesus came into the world to save sinners, of whom I am the foremost" (verse 15).

Both John Newton and the apostle Paul saw themselves as great sinners with a great Savior. Most believers cannot identify with either John Newton or the apostle Paul in the gravity of their earlier sins. We may not have committed adultery, murdered anyone, dealt drugs, or embezzled from our employers. I myself, reflecting back on my life, can say I was usually an obedient child, a model teenager, a trusted employee, and a conscientious husband and father. In fact, I've been on the staff of a Christian ministry for more than fifty years.

However, though I have not committed any of the big scandalous sins, I have gossiped, spoken critically of others, harbored resentment, become impatient, acted selfishly, failed to trust God in difficult issues of life, succumbed to materialism, and even let my favorite football team become an idol. I have to say with Paul that I am the foremost of sinners. Or to paraphrase John Newton's words, "I am a great sinner, but I have a great Savior." That is my only hope. That is the only remedy for my sin, and it is your only remedy as well.

Both John Newton and Paul spoke of themselves as sinners in the present tense. Neither of them said I *was*; they said I *am*. It's clear in the context of Paul's statement that he was reflecting on his earlier sins as a persecutor. Likewise, we know from Newton's own reflections that he never got over the fact that he had been a slave trader. In fact, with each passing year, he became more horrified at his former life.

Does that mean, then, that though describing themselves as sinners in the present tense, they were referring only to their past sins as a persecutor and a slave trader? It is hardly possible that they would think that way. We know, for instance, that several years before writing 1 Timothy, Paul referred to himself as "the very least of all the saints" and as a minister of the gospel only by the grace of God (see Ephesians 3:7-8). In fact, there seems to be a downward progression in Paul's self-awareness from the least of the apostles (see 1 Corinthians 15:9, written in AD 55) to the very least of all the saints (see Ephesians 3:8, written in AD 60) to the foremost of sinners (see 1 Timothy 1:15, written about AD 63 or 64).

We can be sure that over the years from their conversion to their death, both Newton and Paul grew in Christlike character. Over time, both of them acted more and more as the saints they had become at conversion. But that growth process involved becoming more aware of and sensitive to the sinful expressions of the flesh still dwelling within them. And so John Newton could have easily said, "I *was* and *still am* a great sinner, but I have a great Savior." And if you and I are to make any progress in dealing with the acceptable sins of our lives, we must say the same.

The remedy for our sin, whether scandalous or acceptable, is the gospel in its widest scope. The gospel is actually a message; here I am using the word *gospel* as a shorthand expression for the entire work of Christ in His historic life, death, and resurrection for us, and His present work in us through His Holy Spirit. When I say the gospel in its widest scope, I am referring to the fact that Christ, in His work for us and in us, saves us not only from the penalty of sin but also from its dominion or reigning power in our lives. This twofold aspect of Christ's great work is beautifully captured in Augustus Toplady's great hymn "Rock of Ages," with these words:

> Let the water and the blood,
> From thy riven side which flowed,
> Be of sin the double cure,
> Cleanse me from its guilt and power.[2]

We need to take a good look at the gospel. We need to do this for several reasons.

First, the gospel is for sinners. Christ Jesus came into the world to save sinners (see 1 Timothy 1:15). Most Christians tend to think of the gospel as applicable only to unbelievers who need to be "saved." Once we trust in Christ, so the thinking goes, the gospel doesn't apply to us anymore, except to share it with others who are still unbelievers. However, though we truly are saints in the sense of being separated unto God, all of us are still practicing sinners. All the ethical commands and exhortations addressed to believers in the New Testament assume there is still sin present in our lives that needs to be addressed. Among the four uses for which Scripture is profitable, as described in 2 Timothy 3:16, are reproof and correction. Again, these uses assume that we still have sin that needs to be reproved and corrected.

So the first use of the gospel, as a remedy for our sins, is to plow the ground of our hearts so that we can see our sin. Stepping forward to accept our place as sinners in need of the gospel each day drives a dagger into our self-righteous hearts and prepares us to face up to and accept the reality of the sin that still dwells within us.

Second, the gospel not only prepares us to face our sin but also frees us up to do so. Facing our sin causes us to feel guilty. Of course we *feel* guilty because we *are* guilty. And if we believe, consciously or unconsciously, that God still counts our guilt against us, our instinctive sense of self-protection forbids us to acknowledge our sin and guilt, or, at the least, we seek to minimize it. But we cannot begin to deal with a particular manifestation of sin, such as anger or self-pity, until we first openly acknowledge its presence and activity in our lives. So I need the assurance that my sin is forgiven before I can even acknowledge it, let alone begin to deal with it.

By acknowledging my sin, I mean more than a halfhearted admission to myself that I acted selfishly in a given instance. Rather, I mean a wholehearted, defenseless admission, "I am a selfish person, and that particular act was only a manifestation of the selfishness that still dwells within me." But in order to make such an admission, I need the assurance that my selfishness is forgiven — that God no longer holds it against me.

The gospel gives us that assurance. Consider these words from the apostle Paul: "Blessed are those whose lawless deeds are forgiven, and whose sins are covered; blessed is the man against whom the Lord will not count his sin" (Romans 4:7-8).

Why does God not count my sins against me? Because He has already charged it to Christ. To the extent that I grasp, in the depth of my being, this great truth of God's forgiveness of my sin through Christ, I will be freed up to honestly and humbly face the particular manifestations of sin in my life. That's why it is so helpful to affirm each day with John Newton that "I am a great sinner, but I have a great Savior."

Third, the gospel motivates and energizes us to deal with our sin. It is not enough to honestly face our sin. If we are to grow in Christlike character, we must also deal with it. To use a scriptural term, we must put it to death (see Romans 8:13; Colossians 3:5). But as has been well said, the only sin that can be successfully fought against is forgiven sin. We cannot begin to deal with the *activity* of sin in our lives until we have first dealt with its guilt. So here again we go back to the gospel and its assurance that God through Christ has dealt with our guilt.

The assurance that God no longer counts our sin against us does two things. First, it assures us that God is for us, not against us (see Romans 8:31). We are not alone in this battle with sin. God is not watching us from His heavenly throne, saying, "When are you going to get your act together? When are you going to deal with that sin?" Rather, He is coming alongside us, saying, "We are going to work on that sin, but meanwhile I want you to know that I no longer count it against you." God is no longer our judge; He is now our heavenly Father, who loves us with a self-generated, infinite love, even in the face of our sin. That assurance greatly encourages us and motivates us to deal with the sin.

Further, the assurance that God no longer counts our sin against us, and that in our struggles with sin He is for us, produces within us a strong sense of gratitude for what He has done and is presently doing for us through Christ.

This twofold effect of encouragement and gratitude produces in us a *desire* to deal with our sin. Make no mistake: Dealing with our sin is not an option. We are commanded to put sin to death. It is our duty to do so. But duty without desire soon produces drudgery. And it is the truth of the gospel, reaffirmed in our hearts daily, that puts desire into our duty. It is the gospel that stokes the fire of our motivation to deal with our respectable and subtle sins. It is the gospel that motivates us to seek to be in our daily experience what we are in our standing before God.

We can see, then, that the continuous day-by-day appropriation of the gospel, as it assures us of the forgiveness of our sins, is an important part of our dealing with sin in our lives. It is not the only part, but for now, I urge you to commit yourself to a daily, conscious appropriation of the gospel.

The good news that God no longer counts our sin against us, that He has in fact forgiven us of all our sin, is so radical, so contrary to our normal way of thinking, that frankly, it seems too good to be true.

Especially on a day when circumstances have made us vividly aware of our selfishness, impatience, or resentment, it does seem too good to be true.

Whatever Scriptures we use to assure us of God's forgiveness, we must realize that whether the passage explicitly states it or not, the *only* basis for God's forgiveness is the blood of Christ shed on the cross for us. As the writer of Hebrews said, "Without the shedding of blood there is no forgiveness of sins" (9:22), and the context makes it clear that it is Christ's blood that provides the objective basis on which God forgives our sins.

This, then, is the first part of the good news of the gospel: God has forgiven us all our sins through the death of His Son on the cross. To refer back to Toplady's hymn "Rock of Ages," this is the first part of being cleansed of sin's guilt.

The Power of
the Holy Spirit

Augustus Toplady's hymn speaks of the "double cure" — that is, cleansing from both sin's guilt and power. We saw earlier that God does indeed cleanse us from sin's guilt through the death of His Son. God does not forgive because He wants to be lenient with us; He forgives because His justice has been satisfied. The absolute forgiveness of our sins is just as rock solid as the historic reality of Christ's death. It is important that we grasp this wonderful truth of the gospel because we can face our "respectable" sins only when we know they are forgiven.

However, Toplady's hymn speaks of cleansing from not only sin's guilt but also its power. Sometimes when we are struggling with some particular expression of our sin, we wonder if the gospel does address the power of sin in our lives. We wonder if we will ever see progress in putting to death some persistent sin pattern we struggle with. Can we honestly say with Toplady that Christ, the "Rock of Ages," does indeed cleanse us from sin's power as well as its guilt?

To answer that question, we need to see the cleansing from sin's power in two stages. The first is deliverance from the dominion or reigning power of sin that is decisive and complete for all believers. The second is freedom from the remaining presence and activity of sin that is progressive and continues throughout our lives on earth. Paul helps us see this twofold deliverance in Romans 6.

In verse 2, Paul writes that we "died to sin," and in verse 8, he says, "we have died with Christ." Through our union with Christ in His death, we have died not only to sin's guilt but also to its reigning power in our lives. This is true of every believer and is accomplished at the time of our salvation when God delivers us from the domain of darkness and transfers us to the kingdom of His Son (see Colossians 1:13).

Paul's statement that we "died to sin" is a declarative statement. It is something God does for us at the moment of our salvation. Nothing we do subsequent to that decisive transaction can add to or subtract from the fact that we died to both sin's guilt and dominion.

At the same time, however, Paul urges us to "let not sin therefore reign in your mortal body, to make you obey its passions" (Romans 6:12). How can sin possibly reign if we have died to it? Here Paul is referring to the continued presence and ceaseless activity of sin that, though "dethroned" as the reigning power over our lives, still seeks to exert a controlling influence on our daily walk. It continues to wage spiritual guerrilla warfare in our hearts. This warfare is described by Paul in Galatians 5:17:

The desires of the flesh are against the Spirit, and the desires of the Spirit are against the flesh, for these are opposed to each other, to keep you from doing the things you want to do.

We experience this struggle between the desires of the flesh and the desires of the Spirit daily. This tension causes us to sometimes wonder if the gospel really does address this aspect of sin's power to pull us toward its desires. This seems especially true in the more acceptable sins in our lives. Some of these subtle sins seem tenacious and we must battle them daily. With others, we sometimes think we've turned the corner on one, only to discover a few days later that we've just gone around the block and are dealing with it again.

At this point in our struggle, we are prone to think, *It's fine to be told sin no longer has dominion over me, but what about my daily experience of the remaining presence and activity of sin? Does the gospel cleanse me from that? Can I hope to see progress in putting to death the subtle sins of my life?*

Paul's answer is found in Galatians 5:16: "I say, walk by the Spirit, and you will not gratify the desires of the flesh." To walk by the Spirit is to live under the controlling influence of the Spirit and in dependence upon Him. Paul says that as we do this, we will not gratify the desires of the flesh.

Practically speaking, we live under the controlling influence of the Spirit as we continually expose our minds to and seek to obey His moral will for us as revealed in Scripture. We live in dependence on Him through prayer as we continually cry out to Him for His power to enable us to obey His will.

There is a fundamental principle of the Christian life that I call the principle of *dependent responsibility*, which states that we are responsible before God to obey His word by putting to death the sins in our lives, both the so-called acceptable sins and the obviously not acceptable ones. At the same time, we do not have the ability within ourselves to carry out this responsibility. We are in fact totally dependent upon the enabling power of the Holy Spirit. In this sense, we are both responsible and dependent.

As we seek to walk by the Spirit, we will,

over time, see the Spirit working in us and through us to cleanse us from the remaining power of sin in our lives. We will never reach perfection in this life, but we will see progress. It will be incremental progress, to be sure, and sometimes it will appear to be no progress at all. But if we sincerely want to address the subtle sins in our lives, we may be sure the Holy Spirit is at work in us and through us to help us. And we have His promise that "he who began a good work in you will bring it to completion at the day of Jesus Christ" (Philippians 1:6). The Holy Spirit will not abandon the work He has begun in us.

How the Holy Spirit works in us and through us is a mystery in the sense that we cannot comprehend or explain it. We simply accept the testimony of Scripture that He dwells in us and is at work in us to transform us more and more into the likeness of Christ (see 2 Corinthians 3:18). We do need to actively believe this great truth about the Holy Spirit. We need to believe that as we seek to deal with our subtle sins, we are not alone. He is at work in us, and we will see progress as we walk by the Spirit.

One of the ways the Holy Spirit works in us is to bring conviction of sin. He causes us to begin to see our selfishness, impatience, and judgmental attitudes as the sins that they truly are. He works through the Scriptures, which He inspired, to reprove and correct us (see 2 Timothy 3:16). He also works through our consciences, which are enlightened and sensitized by exposure to His Word. I have even known Him to bring to my memory a specific act of a subtle sin and, using that single act as a starting point, begin to point out to me a pattern of that sin in my life. It stands to reason that conviction of sin must be one of His vital works because we cannot begin to deal with a sin, especially one that is common and acceptable in our Christian culture, until we have first realized that the particular pattern of thought, word, or deed is indeed sin.

Another way in which the Holy Spirit works in us is to enable and empower us to deal with our sin. In Romans 8:13, Paul exhorts us *by the Spirit* to "put to death the deeds of the body." In Philippians 2:12-13, he urges us to "work out [our] own salvation . . . for it is God who works in you, both to will and to work for his good pleasure." Paul urges us to work in the confidence that God is at work in us. Though Paul refers to *God*, presumably God the Father, as the One at work, we have already seen that God works through the Holy Spirit as the transforming agent in our lives.

Then Paul says in Philippians 4:13, "I can do all things through him who strengthens me." We can deal with our pride, lust, impatience, and critical and judgmental spirits as we depend on the Holy Spirit to empower and enable us. Thus, we should never give up. Regardless of how little progress we seem to make, He is at work in us. Sometimes He seems to withhold His power, but this may be to cause us to learn experientially that we truly are dependent on Him.

Directions for Dealing with Sin

But we need to do our part, and I want to give some directions for dealing with our "acceptable sins." While there may be particular helps for certain ones, there are general directions that apply to all our subtle sins.

The *first* direction is that we should always address our sin in the context of the gospel. I have covered this truth earlier, but it needs repeating at this point. Our tendency is that as soon as we begin to work on an area of sin in our lives, we forget the gospel. We forget that God has already forgiven us our sin because of the death of Christ. As Paul wrote in Colossians 2:13-14, "[God has] forgiven us all our trespasses, by canceling the record of debt that stood against us with its legal demands. This he set aside, nailing it to the cross."

Not only has God forgiven us our sins, He has also credited to us the perfect righteousness of Christ. In every area of life where we have been disobedient, Jesus was perfectly obedient. Are we prone to be anxious? Jesus always perfectly trusted His heavenly Father. Do we have trouble with selfishness? Jesus was always completely self-giving. Are we guilty of unkind words, gossip, or sarcasm? Jesus spoke only those words that would be appropriate for each occasion. He never once sinned with His tongue.

For some thirty-three years, Jesus lived a life of perfect obedience to the moral will of God, and then He culminated that obedience by being obedient to the Father's specific will for Him — an obedience unto death, even death on the cross for our sins. In both His sinless life and His sin-bearing death, Jesus was perfectly obedient, perfectly righteous, and it is that righteousness that is credited to all who believe (see Romans 3:21-22; Philippians 3:9).

As we struggle to put to death our subtle sins, we must always keep in mind this twofold truth: Our sins are forgiven and we are accepted as righteous by God because of the sinless life and sin-bearing death of our Lord Jesus Christ. There is no greater motivation for dealing with sin in our lives than the realization of these two glorious truths of the gospel.

The *second* direction is that we must learn to rely on the enabling power of the Holy Spirit. Remember, it is by the Spirit that we put to death the sins in our lives (see Romans 8:13). Again, we have already addressed this truth, but as with the gospel, we tend to forget it and resort to our own willpower. It's what I call one of our default settings. Regardless of how much we grow, however, we never get beyond our constant need of the enabling power of the Holy Spirit. Our spiritual lives may be compared to the motor of an electric appliance. The motor does the actual work, but it is constantly dependent upon the external power source of electricity to enable it to work. Therefore, we should cultivate an attitude of continual dependence on the Holy Spirit.

The *third* direction is that while depending on the Holy Spirit, we must at the same time recognize our responsibility to diligently pursue all practical steps for dealing with our sins. I know that keeping both these truths (our dependence and our responsibility) equally in mind is difficult. Our tendency is to emphasize one to the neglect of the other. Here the wisdom of some of the older writers will help us: "Work as if it all depends on you, and yet trust as if you did not work at all."

The *fourth* direction is that we must identify specific areas of acceptable sins. As you think about your daily preoccupations, ask the Holy Spirit to help you see if there is a pattern of sin in your life. This, of course, requires a humble attitude and a willingness to face that sin. As you identify a particular sin, give thought to what situations trigger it. Anticipating the circumstances or events that stimulate the sin can help in putting it to death.

The *fifth* direction is that we should bring to bear specific applicable Scriptures to each of our subtle sins. These Scriptures should be memorized, reflected on, and prayed over as we ask God to use them to enable us to deal with those sins. The psalmist wrote, "I have stored up your word in my heart, that I might not sin against you" (Psalm 119:11). To store up means to lay aside for future need.

Of course, memorizing specific Scripture verses is no magic bullet. They must be applied to our lives. But if we have memorized and prayed over Scriptures that address our subtle sins, the Holy Spirit will bring them to mind in particular situations to remind us of the will of God, to warn us, and to guide us in our response to the temptation.

The *sixth* direction is that we should cultivate the practice of prayer over the sins we tolerate. This is assumed in the second direction about relying on the Holy Spirit and in the fifth direction regarding praying over the Scriptures we memorize. But it is important to single out prayer as one of our major directions for dealing with sin, for it is through prayer that we consciously acknowledge our need of the Holy Spirit, and it is through prayer that we continually acknowledge the presence of those persistent sin patterns in our lives.

Prayers regarding our subtle sins should be of two types. First, we should pray over them in a planned, consistent manner, probably in our daily private time with God. Second, we should pray short, spontaneous prayers for the help of the Holy Spirit each time we encounter situations that might trigger one of our sins.

The *seventh* direction is that we should involve one or more other believers with us in our struggles against our subtle sins. This, of course, should be a mutual relationship as we seek to exhort, encourage, and pray for one another. The Scriptures tell us that "two are better than one, because they have a good reward for their toil. For if they fall, one will lift up his fellow. But woe to him who is alone when he falls and has not another to lift him up!" (Ecclesiastes 4:9-10). We need the mutual vulnerability with and accountability to one another, as well as the praying for one another and encouraging one another, if we want to make progress in dealing with sin.

Romans 8:28 is a text many of us go to for encouragement in tough times. For those who do not recognize the reference, it says, "We know that for those who love God all things work together for good, for those who are called according to his purpose." However, while that passage is indeed one of all-around encouragement to us, Paul is actually talking about our spiritual transformation. The "good" of verse 28 is explained in verse 29 to be conformity to the image of God's Son. This means, then, that the Holy Spirit is at work in us through our circumstances to make us more like Christ.

We do have a vital part to play. We are responsible to put to death the acceptable sins in our lives. We cannot simply lay this responsibility on God and sit back and watch Him work. At the same time, we are dependent; we cannot make one inch of spiritual progress apart from His enabling power.

But the Holy Spirit does more than help us. He is the One actually directing our spiritual transformation. He uses means, of course, and I pray that He will use even this booklet to help us all uncover and deal with the subtle sins in our lives. But He does not leave us to our own insight to see our sins or our own power to deal with them.

So Augustus Toplady's words are true: God does deliver us from both sin's guilt and power through the atoning death of Christ on the cross and the mysterious but very real work of the Holy Spirit in our lives.

Remember, Christ has already paid the penalty for our sins and won for us the forgiveness of them. And then He has sent His Holy Spirit to live within us to enable us to deal with them.

I urge you to pray that the Holy Spirit will enable you to see the hidden, subtle sins in your life. Sin is deceitful (see Ephesians 4:22). It will cause you to live in complete denial of a particular sin or mitigate the seriousness of it. Only the Holy Spirit can successfully expose a sin for what it is.

Notes

1. Brian H. Edwards, *Through Many Dangers: The Story of John Newton* (Welwyn, England: Eurobooks, 1980), 191.
2. An alternate reading of the last phrase is "Save from wrath and make me pure." Of the ten hymnals I consulted, five use the phrase I have used and five use the alternate reading. Either way, the meaning is ultimately the same.

More than 210,000 copies sold— read the entire book now!

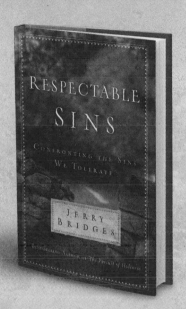

Respectable Sins
Jerry Bridges

If you would like to read more about the "sins you accept," find *Respectable Sins* online or at a bookstore near you.

978-1-60006-140-0

Available wherever books are sold.